I0560782

DESTROYING
EVIL MARKS

DEFEATING YOUR ADVERSARY
IN THE COURTS OF HEAVEN

PRAYER M. MADUEKE

PRAYER
PUBLICATIONS
UNITED STATES

ISBN: 978-1-964584-25-6

Copyright © 2024 Prayer M. Madueke

All rights reserved. No part of this work may be reproduced or transmitted in any form or by any means without written permission from the publisher unless otherwise indicated.

All Scripture quotations are taken from the King James Version of the Bible, and used by permission. All emphasis within quotations is the author's additions.

Published by Prayer Publications.
Printed in the United States of America.

4 Free Ebooks

In order to say a 'Thank You' for purchasing *Destroying Evil Marks*, I offer these books to you in appreciation. Click or type madueke.com/free-gift in your browser.

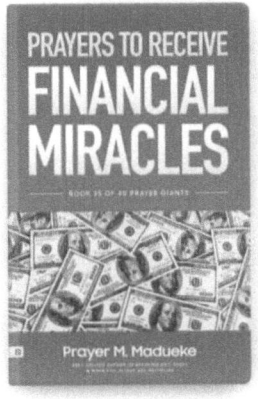

Message from the Author

I want to see you succeed, grow, and break free from negativity and obstacles. My hope is for you to thrive, unaffected by negative influences and challenging situations. Because of that, please permit me to introduce two courses that I believe passionately will help you:

1. To break the evil altars and powers of your father's house, The role of altars in the realm of existence is very key because altars are meeting places between the physical and the spiritual, between the visible and the invisible.

   Unless a man cuts off the evil flow from the power of his father's house, he will not fulfil his destiny. <u>Click here</u> to learn more about <u>my course</u> on how to tear down unholy altars and close the enemy's entryways into your life!

2. To help you seamlessly break iron-like problems, illness, delayed marriage, poverty, or any long-standing battle.

   Discover <u>the transformative power of Christian fasting and prayer</u>. Remember, Matthew 17:21 teaches us, *"But this kind of demon does not go out except by prayer and fasting."* Ready to overcome your struggles? Click here to learn more about this course.

Embrace the journey ahead with faith, for through prayer, fasting, and the dismantling of evil altars, you shall unlock the doors to spiritual liberation and divine breakthrough. May your path be illuminated by His grace as you walk towards a life free from bondage.

If you're seeing this from the physical copy, type the link: madueke.com/courses in your browser to view all the courses on my website.

Prayer Madueke
CHRISTIAN AUTHOR

Christian Counselling

We were created for a greater purpose than only survival and God wants us to live a full life.

If you need prayer or counselling, or if you have any other inquiries, please visit the counselling page on my website to know when I will be available for a phone call.

Click or type links.madueke.com/counselling in your browser.

Let's Connect on Youtube ▶

Join me on my YouTube channel, "Prayer M. Madueke," where I share powerful insights, guidance, and prayers for spiritual breakthroughs.

Subscribe today to unlock the secrets of the Kingdom and embrace an abundant life. Let's grow together!

Click or type links.madueke.com/youtube in your browser.

TABLE OF CONTENTS

ONE

WHAT ARE EVIL MARKS?

A n evil mark is a satanic identification attachment that can easily single a victim out in times of trouble and waste their life without notice.

- It can bring victims into collective bondage or captivity and waste them without negotiation.

And the Gibeonites said unto him, We will have no silver nor gold of Saul, nor of his house; neither for us shalt thou kill any man in Israel. And he said, What ye shall say, that will I do for you. And they answered the king, The man that consumed us, and that devised against us that

we should be destroyed from remaining in any
of the coasts of Israel, Let seven men of his
sons be delivered unto us, and we will hang
them up unto the Lord in Gibeah of Saul, whom
the Lord did choose. And the king said, I will
give them. But the king spared Mephibosheth,
the son of Jonathan the son of Saul, because of
the Lord's oath that was between them,
between David and Jonathan the son of Saul.
But the king took the two sons of Rizpah the
daughter of Aiah, whom she bare unto Saul,
Armoni and Mephibosheth; and the five sons of
Michal the daughter of Saul, whom she brought
up for Adriel the son of Barzillai the Meholathite:
And he delivered them into the hands of the
Gibeonites, and they hanged them in the hill
before the Lord: and they fell all seven together,
and were put to death in the days of harvest, in
the first days, in the beginning of barley
harvest.

— 2 SAMUEL 21:4-9

■ If evil marks are not dealt with, they can waste destinies
when victims need their lives most.

■ Evil marks are very wicked satanic emblems that prevent victims from harvesting what they have planted.

■ In times of action, evil marks expose victims to brutal attacks without mercy.

■ It is important you say these prayers because your deliverance may depend on this matter.

CONSEQUENCES OF EVIL MARKS

■ One of the most effective instruments Satan uses to place evil marks upon people is sin.

■ Though there are other causes like witchcraft attacks, fortune telling, consultations with familiar spirits, magic, palm telling, hypnotism or failure to resist the devil.

Submit yourselves therefore to God. Resist the devil, and he will flee from you.

— JAMES 4:7

- If you open the door of your life through any of the above, the devil and his agents will capitalize on that to mark you with evil manifestations. (John 5:14; 1 Samuel 16:14, 15; 1 Peter 5:8, 9; Ephesians 4:27; Matthew 12:44, 45; James 4:7).

- When Adam and Eve broke the commandment of God by eating the forbidden fruits, the doors of their lives were opened to evil marks. Satan attacked them.

- They became spiritually dead before God.

- Their lives were exposed to demonic attacks and they were enslaved by the devil.

For some are already turned aside after Satan.

— 1 TIMOTHY 5:15

When the unclean spirit is gone out of a man, he walketh through dry places, seeking rest; and finding none, he saith, I will return unto my house whence I came out. And when he cometh, he findeth it swept and garnished.

Then goeth he, and taketh to him seven other
spirits more wicked than himself; and they enter
in, and dwell there: and the last state of that
man is worse than the first.

— LUKE 11:24-26

- Leaving God, seeking for help through evil means, turning to the devil or his agents in search of help attracts evil marks.

- Prayers of deliverance from evil marks are good but it is very dangerous when the delivered refuses to stay with God.

- The reason many pray for deliverance and remain undelivered is because of God's love.

- If God delivers you but you go back to sin, your case will be seven worse than it is at first.

- When Cain cooperated with the devil and began to offer wrong sacrifices like many occult people do today, God warned him against it.

- Instead of repenting and returning God, he tried to force his younger brother to join him in the offering wrong sacrifices.

- Later, he took his brother who sheepishly followed him to a place of evil sacrifice and killed him.
- You may be alive physically but if you have ever followed anyone to a witchcraft or occult group or to a wrong place of sacrifice, you are dead spiritually.

And Nadab and Abihu, the sons of Aaron, took either of them his censer, and put fire therein, and put incense thereon, and offered strange fire before the Lord, which he commanded them not. And there went out fire from the Lord, and devoured them, and they died before the Lord.

— LEVITICUS 10:1-2

- Some ministers or religious leaders have turned places of worship into witchcraft or occult gatherings where strange fires and sacrifices are offered.
- This is why many people in some churches are unconscious witches and wizards.
- They are busy praying and fasting in sin without results.

- Cain killed his brother and when God came to deliver him from evil marks, he started telling lies and asking God useless questions.
- After waiting for his repentance, God withdrew from him and he received the marks of a fugitive and a vagabond under a curse.

And the Lord said unto Cain, Where is Abel thy brother? And he said, I know not: Am I my brother's keeper? And he said, What hast thou done? the voice of thy brother's blood crieth unto me from the ground. And now art thou cursed from the earth, which hath opened her mouth to receive thy brother's blood from thy hand; When thou tillest the ground, it shall not henceforth yield unto thee her strength; a fugitive and a vagabond shalt thou be in the earth.

— GENESIS 4:9-12

- If you ignore God in times of marriage, choose whom to marry by yourself and only invite God to attend your wedding, your marriage will be marked for defeat and failures.

■ This was what the sons of God did and the devil marked them to live in wickedness.

■ Their thoughts were defiled into imagining evil continuously without end. (Genesis 6:1-24).

■ When Reuben, the first son of Jacob, which represented the might of his father and the excellence of his father's dignity and power sinned, he was marked for failure.

■ For years, he had the opportunity to repent and confess to his father and to God but he failed to do so until his father died.

Reuben, thou art my firstborn, my might, and the beginning of my strength, the excellency of dignity, and the excellency of power: Unstable as water, thou shalt not excel; because thou wentest up to thy father's bed; then defiledst thou it: he went up to my couch. And it came to pass, when Israel dwelt in that land, that Reuben went and lay with Bilhah his father's concubine: and Israel heard it. Now the sons of Jacob were twelve.

— GENESIS 49:3, 4; 35:22

- At the time Reuben committed incest with his father's wife, he was full of life and excelled in everything.
- He was comfortable and prosperous from every direction.
- He ignored repentance, confession of his sins and restitution.
- All preaching and counseling to him fell on deaf ears until his father passed on.
- Before his father died, he told Reuben that he will not excel because he went up to his father's couch and defiled it.
- Even after hearing this directly from his father, he went away without saying father I am sorry, forgive me and pray for me.
- He despised the power of repentance and confession of sins.
- Thereafter, he still lived in great wealth and good health but spiritually he was dead without God.

- If only Reuben had foreseen the suffering, hardship, and tears of his unborn generation, he would have humbled himself, repented and confessed his sins.
- The family of King Saul, his children, and all that supported his evil reign suffered except his first son, Jonathan, who was opposed to his wicked reign.

But the king spared Mephibosheth, the son of Jonathan the son of Saul, because of the Lord's oath that was between them, between David and Jonathan the son of Saul. But the king took the two sons of Rizpah the daughter of Aiah, whom she bare unto Saul, Armoni and Mephibosheth; and the five sons of Michal the daughter of Saul, whom she brought up for Adriel the son of Barzillai the Meholathite: And he delivered them into the hands of the Gibeonites, and they hanged them in the hill before the Lord: and they fell all seven together, and were put to death in the days of harvest, in the first days, in the beginning of barley harvest.

— 2 SAMUEL 21:7-9

- The famine that started in the days of David later wiped out the remnant King Saul's bloody family.

- One bad thing about inherited evil is that the victims are destroyed in the prime of life without help.

- When the last messengers of death from the evil carryover (inherited punishment from sins committed by others) arrived at the once busy palace of late King Saul, the men were few.

- These few remaining men were looking haggard, weak and empty of life and despite that, they were handed over to their worst enemy.

- Demons from evil carryover are heartless, merciless, wicked without pity.

- At the beginning of barley harvest after a long time of labor, they were all arrested.

- They were not allowed to eat or rest after harvest but were dragged out and handed over to their enemies.

- They were hanged on the hill before the LORD. They were not secretly killed but openly disgraced in the presence of God.

- Even King David and the soldiers of Israel could not stop their execution in the presence of God.
- If you are suffering now under hardship and hopelessness, prayer is not enough to deliver you.
- You need to acknowledge your sins, repent and confess them.
- You need to make restitution and forsake your sins.

And Samuel spake unto all the house of Israel, saying, If ye do return unto the Lord with all your hearts, then put away the strange gods and Ashtaroth from among you, and prepare your hearts unto the Lord, and serve him only: and he will deliver you out of the hand of the Philistines. Then the children of Israel did put away Baalim and Ashtaroth, and served the Lord only.

— 1 SAMUEL 7:3-4

Therefore pray not thou for this people, neither lift up cry nor prayer for them, neither make intercession to me: for I will not hear thee.

— JEREMIAH 7:16

- Without true repentance, no prayer, fasting, seed of faith and other religious activities can save you from evil carryover.

- After many years, powers of darkness from evil carry-over entered into the family of Reuben and killed off every good thing.

- Before Moses died, he decided to pray for every tribe one after the other and when he saw the tribe of Reuben, he was disappointed.

- When Moses saw what the demons of evil carry-over did in the tribe of Reuben, his prayer was, Let Reuben live, and not die; and let not his men be few (Deuteronomy 33:6).

- To be delivered from evil carry-over, you have to separate yourself from the sins of your ancestors and truly repent. 2 Samuel 3:28, 29.

- You will not only repent and forsake your sins, you have to put on the whole armor of God.

- Demons working from foundations do not easily give up without a battle, direct confrontation and determination for freedom.

- You must know and stand up for your right, fight until you achieve victory.

- Ahab prayed and delivered himself partially from his collective bondage imposed on his family.

- On the other hand, David prayed and delivered himself and his kingdom forever from the crying blood of Abner the son of Ner.

But there was none like unto Ahab, which did sell himself to work wickedness in the sight of the Lord, whom Jezebel his wife stirred up. And he did very abominably in following idols, according to all things as did the Amorites, whom the Lord cast out before the children of Israel. And it came to pass, when Ahab heard those words, that he rent his clothes, and put sackcloth upon his flesh, and fasted, and lay in sackcloth, and went softly. And the word of the Lord came to Elijah the Tishbite, saying, Seest thou how Ahab humbleth himself before me? because he humbleth himself before me, I will not bring the evil in his days: but in his son's days will I bring the evil upon his house.

— 1 KINGS 21:25-29

- The deliverance of Ahab ended in his lifetime but immediately he died, his evil deeds were transferred to his children, even the newborns in his family were wiped out in a moment of time.

- If you cannot deliver your own family, village, community, city or nation, you can deliver yourself from the collective punishment arising from inherited evil and collective bondage.

DECREES TO BE DELIVERED FROM EVIL MARKS

Any evil mark in my body from the water visible or invisible, catch fire, in the name of Jesus. Let the blood of Jesus destroy every mark of the queen of heaven in my life. Let the satanic billboard identifying me with the queen of the coast burn to ashes, in the name of Jesus. Father Lord, break every chain of inherited yokes from marine powers. Every marine spirit pattern of wastage in my place of birth, be frustrated. Father Lord, destroy every evil mark in my life and replace it with your own mark, in the name of Jesus.

Any covenant with the queen of heaven in my life, break by fire, in the name of Jesus. Let the powers of the leviathan working against my promotion die. Blood of Jesus, erase every water spirit mark tormenting my life, in the name of Jesus. Every yoke of destruction from the waters against my life, break, in the name of Jesus. Any evil mark against my marital life, be roasted by fire. Any evil mark assigned to bury my destiny, receive destruction, in the name of Jesus.

I deliver myself completely from every evil identification, in the name of Jesus. O Lord my God, arise in your power and deliver me from collective captivity. Every wicked family spirit exposing me to evil occurrences, die, in the name of Jesus. Any evil power chasing away good things from my life, fall down and die. Holy Ghost fire, burn to ashes every evil mark in my body, in the name of Jesus. Any power from the waters corrupting my life, die suddenly by force. Every chain of suffering destroying my life and family line, break, in the name of Jesus.

O Lord, let your divine pattern substitute evil patterns in my family line, in the name of Jesus. Every arrow of the water spirit fired into my life, break fire. Blood of Jesus, flow into my destiny and spoil every evil mark in my life, in the name of Jesus. My foundation, vomit every evil mark upon my destiny. O Lord, give me victory over every demonic mark upon my life, in the name of Jesus. Anointing to waste the marks of marine spirits fall upon me. Let the evil powers working against God's mark in my life be destroyed, in the name of Jesus.

Any good thing in my life buried by the enemy be resurrected, in the name of Jesus. Every manifestation of evil marks in my body, disappear forever. I command the fire of God to burn to ashes every evil mark upon my life, in the name of Jesus. Any power causing evil marks to prosper in my body. Any evil power assigned to expose me to shame, be disgraced, in the name of Jesus. Every effect of evil marks upon my life, disappear forever. Arrows of evil marks upon my life, locate your senders by fire, in the name of Jesus.

Lord Jesus, command deliverance to take place in my life, in the name of Jesus. Any evil mark corrupting my destiny, die by force. Any damage done by evil marks upon my life, be roasted by fire, in the name of Jesus. O Lord, end all the activities of evil marks upon my life. You my life, jump out from every evil mark against you, in the name of Jesus. Wherever evil marks are hiding in my body, fire of God, burn them. Any evil mark in my career or business, die, in the name of Jesus.

Let all demonic assignments in my life be terminated, in the name of Jesus. Holy Ghost fire, withdraw my destiny from all evil marks. I stand against every demonic mark from the waters, in the name of Jesus. Lord Jesus, take away every stubborn mark upon my life. Any strange fire brought by evil marks upon my life, be quenched, in the name of Jesus. Let the mark of the serpent in my body be roasted by fire. Ancient of Days, deliver me from all demonic marks of destruction, in the name of Jesus.

Every poison of the serpent upon my life, dry. Let the ancient mark of the devil in me die by fire, in the name of Jesus.

T W O

DELIVERANCE FROM INHERITED CURSES

I nherited curses are very dangerous and destructive. To be labor under a curse means to be placed out of the reach of blessings and the good things of life. It means to be and remain under the control of evil wishes and demonic utterance. It means to be in a satanic vehicle that drives a person to problems, sorrows, and calamities.

> Manasseh was twelve years old when he began
> to reign, and reigned fifty and five years in
> Jerusalem. And his mother's name was
> Hephzibah. And he did that which was evil in the

sight of the Lord, after the abominations of the heathen, whom the Lord cast out before the children of Israel. For he built up again the high places which Hezekiah his father had destroyed; and he reared up altars for Baal, and made a grove, as did Ahab king of Israel; and worshipped all the host of heaven, and served them.

— 2 KINGS 21:1-3

Being cursed means living under the control of a spell, battling with demonic barriers or invisible enemies that keep people away from good things. The reason for this prayer is to destroy every acquired and inherited curse. (Lamentations 5:7-12).

It is time to say no to poverty. It is time to break the yoke of suffering and hardship. It is time to break loose from the control of evil utterances, demonic characters, witchcraft spells, evil activators, and walk back to our divinely-ordained destinies.

It is good for a man that he bear the yoke in his youth. I called upon thy name, O Lord, out of the low dungeon. Thou hast heard my voice: hide not thine ear at my breathing, at my cry.

— LAMENTATIONS 3:27, 55-56

As we go into these prayers, we shall be discharged from evil mobility; freed from disgrace, released from ancestral evil hold, delivered from disfavor, and walk back to God's original plan for our lives. Pray hard and the Lord will not say no to your request.

DECREES TO BE DELIVERED FROM INHERITED CURSES

Father Lord, arise and destroy every inherited hardship in my life in the name of Jesus. Every inherited poverty in my life, die. I command the yoke of inherited late marriage in my life to break, in the name of Jesus. O Lord, take away from my life every inherited curse. Father Lord, destroy the inherited barrenness in my life, in the name of Jesus. Every inherited evil character in my life, die. Let all inherited witchcraft about to waste my destiny be wasted in the name of Jesus.

Every inherited curse in my life from marine spirits, I reject you completely in the name of Jesus. Evil activators upon my destiny, die. Let all inherited sickness assigned to kill me die in the name of Jesus. I reject every inherited untimely death working against my destiny. Father Lord, destroy every inherited failure assigned to frustrate me, in the name of Jesus. Every inherited curse upon my business, die. Every cobweb of disfavor upon my life, receive fire, in the name of Jesus.

Every inherited iron-like curse, be cut into pieces, in the name of Jesus. Father Lord, deliver me from every generational curse.

Every curse that has arrested everyone in my family line, release me by force. Every Stubborn curse from my ancestors, release me immediately, in the name of Jesus. Every arrow of curse fired into my life, go back by fire now. Any evil sacrifice invoking parental curse against me, expire, in the name of Jesus. O Lord, discharge me from the consequences of inherited curses. All multiple curses from my ancestors assigned to disgrace me, die. Blood of Jesus, speak for my deliverance from every inherited curse, in the name of Jesus.

THREE

BREAKING EVIL COVENANTS

C ovenants are made between nations. It is defined as a
legal contract one enters into and by which his course
of actions is bound. A covenant can be between man and
woman or God and man. When it is between a man and an evil
spirit, it is called an evil covenant. When it is between an
ungodly person, nation and God's children, it brings problems.

> And Joshua made peace with them, and made a
> league with them, to let them live: and the
> princes of the congregation sware unto them.
> And Joshua called for them, and he spake unto
> them, saying, Wherefore have ye beguiled us,

saying, We are very far from you; when ye dwell among us? Now therefore ye are cursed, and there shall none of you be freed from being bondmen, and hewers of wood and drawers of water for the house of my God. And Joshua made them that day hewers of wood and drawers of water for the congregation, and for the altar of the Lord, even unto this day, in the place which he should choose.

— JOSHUA 9:15, 22-23, 27

Evil covenants can bring their victims premature death, non-achievement, and poverty. They can mark their victims with hatred and rejection. They can also bring victims into spells, and cause destruction, mental problems, accidents, sorrow, and mysterious problems.

Then there was a famine in the days of David three years, year after year; and David enquired of the Lord. And the Lord answered, It is for Saul, and for his bloody house, because he slew the Gibeonites. And the king called the Gibeonites, and said unto them; (now the

Gibeonites were not of the children of Israel, but of the remnant of the Amorites; and the children of Israel had sworn unto them: and Saul sought to slay them in his zeal to the children of Israel and Judah.) Wherefore David said unto the Gibeonites, What shall I do for you? and wherewith shall I make the atonement, that ye may bless the inheritance of the Lord?

— 2 SAMUEL 21:1-3

As you engage in these prayers, the Lord will arise and break every evil covenant in your life, deliver your destiny from destruction, and energize you to live above evil occurrences.

DECREES TO BREAK EVIL COVENANTS

Father Lord, arise in your power and break every evil covenant against my life, in the name of Jesus. O hand of God, break every marine covenant working against my destiny. Any evil covenant causing me to come last in every competition, break, in the name of Jesus. Let every ancestral covenant activating poverty in my life break by fire. Any evil covenant energizing sin in my life, break. Let the covenant of the enemy in my life promoting impossibilities be broken, in the name of Jesus.

Let the evil covenant in my life assisting evil to prosper in my life break, in the name of Jesus. Evil covenant of late marriage in my family, break by fire. Every covenant of bad behaviors in my lineage, break by force, in the name of Jesus. Every covenant of barrenness in my life, break and die forever. Every demonic covenant keeping me in the bondage of poverty, break, in the name of Jesus. Every evil covenant in my life leading me to untimely death, break. Let every satanic covenant assigned to steal my peace break, in the name of Jesus.

Blood of Jesus, arise and break the covenant of failure in my life, in the name of Jesus. Father Lord, frustrate every evil covenant causing people to reject me. Heavenly Father, destroy every evil covenant promoting miscarriage in my life. Any evil covenant in my family attacking me with fear, break, in the name of Jesus. Father Lord, arise in your power and break the covenant of Satan in my life, in the name of Jesus. Any ancestral covenant causing me to be disfavored, break now. Covenant of marital breakup in my family, break, in the name of Jesus.

Any evil covenant promoting backwardness in my life, break, in the name of Jesus. Let every ancient covenant causing me to labor in vain break by force. Demons attacking my destiny as a result of evil covenant, die, in the name of Jesus. Blood of Jesus, speak my destiny out of evil covenant, in the name of Jesus. Let the anger of the Lord break every evil covenant working against me. Lord Jesus, break evil covenants in my life that is taking me backward, in the name of Jesus.

Every covenant of non-achievement in my life, break, in the name of Jesus. Holy Ghost fire, burn to ashes every evil covenant attacking me. Blood of Jesus, locate and destroy every evil hidden covenant, in the name of Jesus. Covenant of evil patterns in my life break by fire. Any evil covenant in my family attacking my career, break, in the name of Jesus. Let my God arise and break every covenant of false religion in my life, in the name of Jesus. Any evil covenant bringing evil appetite into my life, break. I break every evil covenant attacking me from the waters. O Lord, arise and deliver me from curses from evil covenants, in the name of Jesus.

Every covenant of hardship that has refused to let me go, break, in the name of Jesus. Every evil covenant in my life causing me to suffer setbacks, break. Holy Ghost fire, burn to ashes every evil covenant in my life, in the name of Jesus. Any sickness in my life because of evil covenant, break. Any demonic infirmity progressing in my life because of evil covenant, die, in the name of Jesus. Every satanic embargo placed upon my life because of evil covenant, be lifted now. Any marine covenant bringing me back to square one, break now. O Lord my God, destroy every evil covenant in my life perfectly, in the name of Jesus.

FOUR

SILENCING EVIL BLOOD

One of the greatest enemies of our generation is the cry of evil blood. Evil blood can cry from our foundation if they are not silenced. Evil blood is a very dangerous voice and an effective demonic weapon that can destroy people's greatness. The consequences of evil blood are many. Evil blood can discover people's destiny and destroy them. They can bring affliction, oppression, and help people to take wrong decisions in life. Evil blood can capture people's stars and progress and waste them. Evil blood can halt people's progress, mark people with an evil mark of rejection and close people's doors to opportunities. But I have good news for you: Evil blood can be silenced by the blood of Jesus.

And to Jesus the mediator of the new
covenant, and to the blood of sprinkling, that
speaketh better things than that of Abel.

— HEBREWS 12:24

And afterward when David heard it, he said, I
and my kingdom are guiltless before the Lord
for ever from the blood of Abner the son of
Ner: Let it rest on the head of Joab, and on all
his father's house; and let there not fail from the
house of Joab one that hath an issue, or that is
a leper, or that leaneth on a staff, or that falleth
on the sword, or that lacketh bread.

— 2 SAMUEL 3:28-29

If you know how to use the blood of Jesus, your problems are
over. The blood of Jesus can fight your battles, silence evil blood
and speak peace into your life.

DECREES TO SILENCE EVIL BLOOD

Any evil blood crying in my foundation, be silenced by the blood of Jesus, in the name of Jesus. Any blood of abortion crying against my marriage, drink the blood of Jesus and stop your crying. Any evil blood promoting barrenness in my life, shut up by the blood of Jesus. Father Lord, stop the cries of evil blood against my destiny today, in the name of Jesus. Any crying blood promoting poverty in my life, be silenced by the blood of Jesus. Any devastating cry of blood energizing premature death in my family, die, in the name of Jesus.

Blood of Jesus, arise and cry 24 hours for my perfect deliverance, in the name of Jesus. Blood of Jesus, speak complete liberty into my destiny. Blood of Jesus, speak victory into my life against evil crying blood, in the name of Jesus. Any evil blood crying against my life, be silenced by the blood of Jesus, in the name of Jesus. I soak my destiny with the blood of Jesus. I plead the blood of Jesus against every crying blood in my life. Every stubborn problem in my life, drink the blood of Jesus and die, in the name of Jesus.

Oppressors of my destiny, be oppressed by the blood of Jesus, in the name of Jesus. Any evil blood crying against me in this area, be stopped by the blood of Jesus. I command every evil blood speaking against me in this house to be silenced by the blood of Jesus, in the name of Jesus. Blood of Jesus, speak destruction to the evil voice attacking me in this office. Every voice of the innocent ones crying against me in this village/area, etc., I close your mouth with the blood of Jesus, in the name of Jesus.

Any sickness that evil blood has put into my life, die by the blood of Jesus, in the name of Jesus. Blood of Jesus, overtake every evil blood crying against me in this land. I overcome every problem in my life by the blood of Jesus, in the name of Jesus. Every blood covenant disgracing my life, be broken by the blood of Jesus. Blood of Jesus, remove every curse placed upon my life. I break away and loose myself from the bloodshed crying against my life, in the name of Jesus.

I hold the blood of Jesus against all the crying blood sacrifice in this land, in the name of Jesus. You the foundation of this land, drink the blood of Jesus. Any evil altar harboring evil blood against my life, scatter by thunder, in the name of Jesus. Let the blood of Jesus, frustrate every evil crying blood against me. You occult grand masters invoking evil blood against my life, be confused by the blood of Jesus. By the power in the blood of Jesus, I close the mouths of every evil crying blood against me, in the name of Jesus.

Every work of darkness against my life, be terminated by the blood of Jesus, in the name of Jesus. Every device of the wicked, be frustrated by the blood of Jesus. Angry blood of Jesus, deliver me from every crying blood against me, in the name of Jesus. Any evil blood covenant, crying against me die and die again. Let every satanic door opened by evil blood against me be closed forever, in the name of Jesus. Eternal rock of ages, use the blood of Jesus to terminate every problem in my life. Blood of Jesus, dry up every evil blood in my root, in the name of Jesus.

Any evil sacrifice against me in the past, expire by the blood of Jesus, in the name of Jesus. Any evil blood crying against me from the grave, die. Any evil blood calling my name from the cemetery, be silenced. Any hidden blood covenant working against my destiny, be silenced immediately, in the name of Jesus. Heavenly Father, pour down the blood of your son Jesus Christ for my sake. Blood of Jesus, locate my stubborn enemy for judgment, in the name of Jesus. Any curse upon my life, blood of Jesus, cancel it by force. Any crying blood from the waters, be silenced by force now, in the name of Jesus.

Let every crying blood attacking my life from the heavenly places stop, in the name of Jesus. Crying blood of Jesus, outcry every evil blood for my sake. I hold the blood of Jesus, and I silence every problem in my life; past, present, and future, in the name of Jesus.

FIVE

MY DESTINY, APPEAR!

T o live life on earth without fulfilling your destiny is a great loss. Yet millions of people on earth are living without discovering their destinies. It is possible to be born on this earth, live, and die without operating in the fullness of your destiny (Acts 26:14-19).

Paul made great achievements on earth. He had confidence in the flesh. He was circumcised on the eight day and was of the stock of Israel from the tribe of Benjamin. He was a Hebrew of Hebrews and a great Pharisee. He was a great scholar and a zealous man, but he was yet to discover his destiny until he met Christ.

And when we were all fallen to the earth, I heard a voice speaking unto me, and saying in the Hebrew tongue, Saul, Saul, why persecutest thou me? it is hard for thee to kick against the pricks. And I said, Who art thou, Lord? And he said, I am Jesus whom thou persecutest. But rise, and stand upon thy feet: for I have appeared unto thee for this purpose, to make thee a minister and a witness both of these things which thou hast seen, and of those things in the which I will appear unto thee; Delivering thee from the people, and from the Gentiles, unto whom now I send thee, To open their eyes, and to turn them from darkness to light, and from the power of Satan unto God, that they may receive forgiveness of sins, and inheritance among them which are sanctified by faith that is in me. Whereupon, O king Agrippa, I was not disobedient unto the heavenly vision:

— ACTS 26:14-19

His life started functioning before God when he came in contact with the saving power of Jesus. You may even be a Christian and yet not have discovered your destiny. If that is your case, you need to pray these prayers. If you handle these prayers aggressively as a Christian, the eaters of your destiny will bow and your full destiny will appear. The deliverance fire of God will deliver your destiny from captivity and set you free.

DECREES TO DISCOVER YOUR DESTINY

Eaters of destiny, listen to me carefully; you shall not eat up my destiny, in the name of Jesus. Destroyers of destiny, my destiny is not your candidate; fail woefully. Blood of Jesus, speak strength into my weak destiny, in the name of Jesus. Deliverance fire of God, arise and deliver my destiny. Every evil decree against my destiny, be revoked by fire. O Lord, release my destiny from every prison yard, in the name of Jesus. Heavenly Father, frustrate every destiny killer assigned against my destiny. My destiny, arise and shine by fire, in the name of Jesus.

Lord Jesus, you will not watch the enemy destroy my great destiny, in the name of Jesus. Destiny destroyers assigned to waste my marriage, be wasted. Every yoke upon my life to destroy my destiny, break, in the name of Jesus. Yoke of iniquity commissioned to destroy my destiny, break by force. Any satanic agent that has vowed to destroy my destiny, be destroyed. Every demon of marital breakup that has vowed to finish me through my marriage, die. Any power limiting my destiny, you are a liar; release it now, in the name of Jesus.

Any satanic altar that has arrested my destiny, scatter by thunder, in the name of Jesus.

My original, wherever you are, appear in the name of Jesus. Any power that has vowed to bring my destiny back to square one, die, in the name of Jesus. Every arrow of death fired against my destiny, backfire. Any infirmity placed upon my destiny, die, in the name of Jesus. Environmental forces fighting to destroy my destiny, catch fire and die. O Lord, arise in your anger and destroy the enemies of my destiny. Any power, causing rising and falling upon my destiny, be detained unto death, in the name of Jesus.

Let the spirit of fear upon my destiny die, in the name of Jesus. Father Lord, cast out every spirit of untimely death upon my destiny. Ancestral power of poverty, waging war against my destiny, be defeated, in the name of Jesus. Anointing of memory failure upon my destiny, I cast you out. Fire of God, possess my destiny every day, in the name of Jesus. Every demonic spirit of non-achievement upon my destiny, I cast you out. Any bad character about to waste my destiny, be roasted by fire, in the name of Jesus.

Any witchcraft attacks against my destiny, be terminated, in the name of Jesus. Any inherited evil, frustrating my destiny, I reject you. Every satanic curse upon my destiny, die by fire, in the name of Jesus. Let all evil covenants that are militating against my destiny break. Any power from the pit of hell monitoring my destiny for evil, be blinded. Any demonic fear that has taken over my destiny, release it and die, in the name of Jesus. Every yoke of impossibility against my destiny, break. Arrows of hardship fired against my destiny, backfire, in the name of Jesus.

Every problem that has gripped my destiny unto death, be roasted by fire, in the name of Jesus. Arrows of hardship fired unto my destiny, I fire you back by force. You my spirit wife/husband attacking my destiny, I break your marriage with me, in the name of Jesus. You my destiny, appear by force and receive power to prosper. Any yoke of rejection upon my destiny, break now, in the name of Jesus. Blood of Jesus, erase every evil mark upon my destiny. Owners of the evil load upon my destiny, appear and carry your load, in the name of Jesus. You my stolen destiny, I recover you by force. Father Lord, search the land of the living and the dead and recover my destiny completely, in the name of Jesus.

THANK YOU!

I'd like to use this time to thank you for purchasing my books and helping my ministry and work. Any copy of my book you buy helps to fund my ministry and family, as well as offering much-needed inspiration to keep writing. My family and I are very thankful, and we take your assistance very seriously.

You have already accomplished so much, but I would appreciate an honest review of some of my books through the link below. This is critical since reviews reflect how much an author's work is respected.

Please [click here] to leave a review on Amazon. If you're viewing from a printed version, please visit amazon.com/review/create-review?asin=B096CPJYX3 to leave a review.

Please be aware that I read and value all comments and reviews. You can always post a review even though you haven't finished the book yet, and then edit your reviews later.

Thank you so much as you spare a precious moment of your time and may God bless you and meet you at the very point of your need.

You can also send me an email to hello@madueke.com if you encounter any difficulty while writing your review.

PRAYER M. MADUEKE'S BESTSELLING BOOKS

Click on any of the [Buy Now] buttons to view or purchase them on my website. If you're viewing from a printed version, please visit madueke.com and search for these books.

1.	Dictionary of Demons & Complete Deliverance	[Buy Now]
2.	Monitoring Spirits	[Buy Now]
3.	Praying with The Blood of Jesus	[Buy Now]
4.	The Power of Speaking in Tongues	[Buy Now]
5.	Speaking Things into Existence by Faith	[Buy Now]
6.	Discerning and Defeating the Ahab & Jezebel Spirit	[Buy Now]
7.	Defeating the Python Spirit	[Buy Now]
8.	35 Special Dangerous Decrees	[Buy Now]
9.	21/40 Nights of Decrees and Your Enemies Will Surrender	[Buy Now]

10. Command the Morning, Day and Night [Buy Now]

11. Evil Summon [Buy Now]

12. Overcoming & Destroying the Spirit of
Rejection & Hatred [Buy Now]

13. Queen of Heaven: Wife of Satan [Buy Now]

14. The False Prophet [Buy Now]

15. Dominion Over Sickness & Disease [Buy Now]

16. The Battle Plan for Destroying
Foundational Witchcraft [Buy Now]

17. The Queen of the Coast [Buy Now]

18. Dictionary of Unmerited Favor [Buy Now]

19. Prayers for Breakthrough in your Business [Buy Now]

20. A Jump From Evil Altar [Buy Now]

21. 100 Days Prayers to Wake Up Your
Lazarus [Buy Now]

22. Breaking Evil Yokes [Buy Now]

23. When Evil Altars are Multiplied   [**Buy Now**]

24. The Battle Plan for Destroying Foundational Occultism   [**Buy Now**]

25. Prayers for Protection   [**Buy Now**]

26. Prayers for Academic Success   [**Buy Now**]

27. Your Dream Directory   [**Buy Now**]

28. Prayers for Financial Breakthrough   [**Buy Now**]

29. Destiny and Star Hunters   [**Buy Now**]

30. Prayers to Pray during Courtship   [**Buy Now**]

31. 91 Days Decrees to Takeover the Year   [**Buy Now**]

32. Alone with God   [**Buy Now**]

33. Prayers against Satanic Oppression   [**Buy Now**]

34. Foundations Exposed   [**Buy Now**]

35. Prayers for Deliverance   [**Buy Now**]

36. Prayers to Heal Broken Relationship   [**Buy Now**]

4 Free Ebooks

In order to say a 'Thank You' for purchasing *Destroying Evil Marks*, I offer these books to you in appreciation. Click or type **madueke.com/free-gift** in your browser.

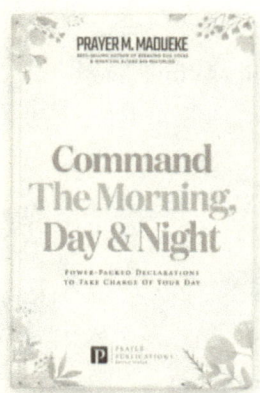

Video Bonus

I've created exclusive video content to complement the topics covered in the book. These videos provide deeper insights and discussions on the things discussed in this book, offering you a more immersive learning experience.

To access the video bonus for this course, simply click or type links.madueke.com/35DEM in your browser.

Message from the Author

I want to see you succeed, grow, and break free from negativity and obstacles. My hope is for you to thrive, unaffected by negative influences and challenging situations. Because of that, please permit me to introduce two courses that I believe passionately will help you:

1. To break the evil altars and powers of your father's house, The role of altars in the realm of existence is very key because altars are meeting places between the physical and the spiritual, between the visible and the invisible.

   Unless a man cuts off the evil flow from the power of his father's house, he will not fulfil his destiny. **Click here** to learn more about **my course** on how to tear down unholy altars and close the enemy's entryways into your life!

2. To help you seamlessly break iron-like problems, illness, delayed marriage, poverty, or any long-standing battle.

   Discover **the transformative power of Christian fasting and prayer**. Remember, Matthew 17:21 teaches us, *"But this kind of demon does not go out except by prayer and* *fasting."* Ready to overcome your struggles? <u>Click here</u> to learn more about this course.

Embrace the journey ahead with faith, for through prayer, fasting, and the dismantling of evil altars, you shall unlock the doors to spiritual liberation and divine breakthrough. May your path be illuminated by His grace as you walk towards a life free from bondage.

If you're seeing this from the physical copy, type the link: <u>madueke.com/courses</u> in your browser to view all the courses on my website.

Prayer Madueke
CHRISTIAN AUTHOR

Christian Counselling

We were created for a greater purpose than only survival and God wants us to live a full life.

If you need prayer or counselling, or if you have any other inquiries, please visit the counselling page on my website to know when I will be available for a phone call.

Click or type **links.madueke.com/counselling** in your browser.

Let's Connect on Youtube ▶

Join me on my YouTube channel, "Prayer M. Madueke," where I share powerful insights, guidance, and prayers for spiritual breakthroughs.

Subscribe today to unlock the secrets of the Kingdom and embrace an abundant life. Let's grow together!

Click or type links.madueke.com/youtube in your browser.

An Invitation to Become a Ministry Partner

I appreciate the support and inquiries I have received regarding collaboration with my ministry. Your prayers and dedication to the work of the Kingdom are highly valued.

You can also visit the donation page on my website if you would like to contribute or learn more about supporting my ministry: madueke.com/donate.

Thank you for your continued support and faithfulness in Christ Jesus.

www.ingramcontent.com/pod-product-compliance
Lightning Source LLC
Chambersburg PA
CBHW031235120626
46545CB00003B/1129